DATE DUE

The Wonder of
MOOSE

ANIMAL WONDERS

ANIMAL WONDERS

ANIMAL WONDERS

ANIMAL WONDERS

ANIMAL WONDERS • ANIMAL WONDERS •

For all my Sister's children.   — Jeff Fair

For a free color catalog describing Gareth Stevens' list of high-quality books and multimedia programs, call 1-800-542-2595 (USA) or 1-800-461-9120 (Canada). Gareth Stevens Publishing's Fax: (414) 225-0377. See our catalog, too, on the World Wide Web: http://gsinc.com

Library of Congress Cataloging-in-Publication Data

Ritchie, Rita.
    The wonder of moose / by Rita Ritchie and Jeff Fair ; photographs by Michael H. Francis ; illustrations by Sandy Stevens.
        p. cm. — (Animal wonders)
    "Based on . . . Moose magic for kids . . . by Jeff Fair"—T.p. verso.
    Includes index.
    Summary: Text and photographs introduce a huge animal of the north woods.
    ISBN 0-8368-1561-0 (lib. bdg.)
    1. Moose—Juvenile literature. [1. Moose.] I. Fair, Jeff.
II. Francis, Michael H. (Michael Harlowe), 1953- ill. III. Stevens, Sandy, ill.
IV. Fair, Jeff. Moose. V. Title. VI. Series.
QL737.U55R58   1996
599.73'57--dc20   96-5001

First published in North America in 1996 by
Gareth Stevens Publishing
1555 North RiverCenter Drive, Suite 201
Milwaukee, WI 53212 USA

This edition is based on the book *Moose Magic for Kids* © 1992 by Jeff Fair, first published in the United States in 1992 by NorthWord Press, Inc., Minocqua, Wisconsin, and published in a library edition by Gareth Stevens, Inc., in 1995. All photographs © 1992 by Michael H. Francis, except pp. 6, 10, 28, 44 © Robert W. Baldwin, with illustrations by Sandy Stevens. Additional end matter © 1996 by Gareth Stevens, Inc.

Printed in the United States of America

1 2 3 4 5 6 7 8 9 99 98 97 96

The Wonder of
MOOSE

by Rita Ritchie and Jeff Fair
Photographs by Michael H. Francis
Illustrations by Sandy Stevens

Gareth Stevens Publishing
MILWAUKEE

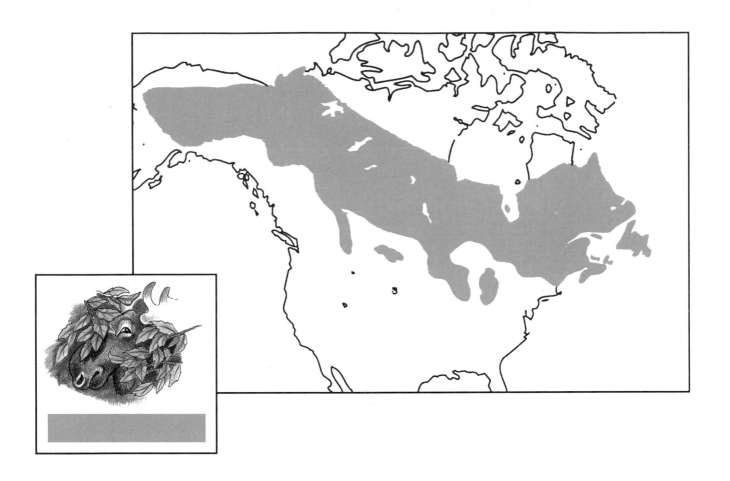

Moose live in the great
north woods that grow
across North America
from Alaska to Maine.

Moose eat the plants growing in marshes, bogs, lakes, and clearings in the woods.

In the past, American Indians made clothes and shelter from moose hides. They made tools from the bones and antlers. They ate moose meat all winter.

People
still hunt
moose.
But moose
are hard
to find
deep in
the woods.

A male moose is called a
bull. It has big antlers and
a skin flap, called a dewlap,
on its throat.

Moose stand
6 feet (1.8 meters)
tall at the
shoulder and
weigh about
1,000 pounds
(454 kilograms).
That's heavier
than four
refrigerators.

Moose tracks look
like teardrops.

Moose eat plants in summer and tree bark in winter.  Droppings are soft and large in summer and hard and small in winter.

Moose like to sleep in clearings called meadows. They trample tall grass for a soft bed.

In spring,
moose
eat leaves
and twigs.
Because
moose have
long legs,
it is hard
for them
to reach
down and
eat grass.

A moose has front teeth only
on its bottom jaw. It uses
these teeth to scrape
the bark off trees.

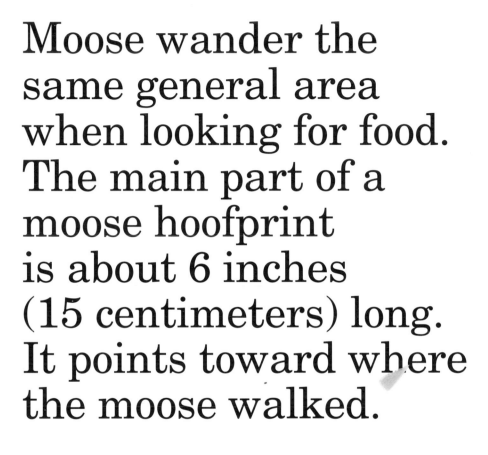

Moose wander the same general area when looking for food. The main part of a moose hoofprint is about 6 inches (15 centimeters) long. It points toward where the moose walked.

A female moose, called a cow, has a calf each May or June. The newborn calf weighs from 25 to 35 pounds (11 to 16 kg).

The cow defends her calf from bears and wolves. She puts her ears back, lowers her head, and charges. She also kicks.

Moose shed their thick winter
coats in spring. In fall, they grow
new winter coats of woolly fur,
covered by long, bristly hairs.

Flies and mosquitoes swarm the woods when it is warm. Moose escape them by moving into the water.

Moose can dive 18 feet (5.5 m) into water to eat juicy pond weeds. Valves in a moose's nose keep water out of the nose. Each mother moose teaches her calf how to swim and what plants to eat.

Moose can step over most objects. Their long legs also help them run fast through deep water, mud, or snow. If a moose gets stuck, it rests a while, and then works its way loose. Moose can run up to 35 miles (56 km) an hour.

Beavers cut down and eat
the same trees moose feed on.
Moose cool off in the beaver
ponds. When the beavers
move on, new trees grow.

Like other ruminants, a moose has four stomachs. It fills the first stomach with 50 pounds (23 kg) of food a day and brings it up later to chew again.

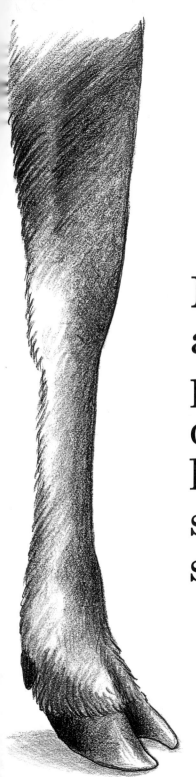

Moose have good eyesight and hearing. They can pick up the faintest scent of another animal or human. Then they sneak silently into the forest shadows to hide.

31

In summer, the young bulls grow a single antler, called a spike. Older bulls grow branching antlers over 6 feet (1.8 m) across that weigh 75 pounds (34 kg). Soft skin, called velvet, covers the growing antlers.

A newborn moose stays with its mother until the following spring. During its first summer, the calf grows quickly. By fall, it may weigh as much as 400 pounds (180 kg).

During breeding season, bull moose make a big bellowing sound to call to other moose.

In late fall, bull moose fight
each other with their big
antlers for mates. The moose
will shed their antlers later.

While two bulls fight, the cow waits near-by. The bull that wins the fight will mate with the cow.

39

In moose country, winter is very cold. When snow gets deep, moose gather together and stay in groups. They find shelter in clusters of fir trees and sleep in the snow. Their heavy winter coats help keep them warm.

In spring, cows give birth.
Then, their older calves,
or yearlings, begin to live
on their own.

Moose often wander onto the roads in spring. They like the salt that was spread there during winter.

About one million moose live in North America today. They face many dangers. People hunt them. Bears and wolves eat moose calves. Parasites called brain worms kill moose. They get the worms from deer.

Sometimes a curious moose will come up to a cabin in the woods. The people inside the cabin are  lucky to get a close-up view of the moose before it trots back into the woods.

A long time ago, American Indians gave the moose its name. *Moose* means "he who eats of trees and shrubs" or "twig-eater." The Indians believed that moose were a good sign. They said that people who often dream of moose will live a long life.

Glossary

antler – a bony growth on the heads of various animals, such as moose and deer

dewlap – a loose fold of skin hanging under the neck of certain animals, such as moose

mates – two animals, one female and one male, that join together to produce young

parasite – an animal or plant that gets its nourishment by living in or on another animal or plant

ruminants – hoofed animals that have three or four stomachs. Ruminants chew their cud as part of digesting food

spike – the single antler found on a young bull moose

velvet – the soft skin that covers and nourishes developing antlers

yearling – an animal that is one year old or in its second year of life

Index